Mindfulness

calm Kids

By
William Anthony

BEARPORT
PUBLISHING

Minneapolis, Minnesota

Library of Congress Cataloging-in-Publication Data is available at www.loc.gov or upon request from the publisher.

ISBN: 978-1-64747-564-2 (hardcover)
ISBN: 978-1-64747-569-7 (paperback)
ISBN: 978-1-64747-574-1 (ebook)

© 2021 Booklife Publishing
This edition is published by arrangement with Booklife Publishing.

For more information, write to Bearport Publishing, 5357 Penn Avenue South, Minneapolis, MN 55419. Printed in the United States of America.

Photo Credits. All images courtesy of Shutterstock. With thanks to Getty Images, Thinkstock Photo, and iStockphoto. Recurring images: Abscent (pattern from cover), ag1100 (paper texture), Puslatronik (font), Sopelkin (doodle embellishments), Amy Li (illustrations and doodles). Cover - Jaromir Chalabala, wk1003mike, 32 pixels, p1 - Jaromir Chalabala, p2-3 - Rido, p4-5 - Samuel Borges Photography, Sunny studio, p6-7 - Monkey Business Images, Aleksandra Suzi, p8-9 - GOLFX, LightField Studios, p10-11 - wavebreakmedia, Creativa Images, p12-13 - Evgeny Atamanenko, p14-15 - Ann in the uk, Elenamiv, Kriengsuk Prasroetsung, Sergey Novikov, p16-17 - vystekimages, DeeMPhotography, p18-19 - Tatyana Vyc, New Africa, Dmytro Zinkevych, p20-21 - leadenpork, shanshinyury, p22-23 - KAMPUS, Asier Romero, wk1003mike, Pixel-Shot, aekkorn

Contents

Healthy You

Keeping your body **healthy** can mean lots of different things. It can mean eating right, exercising, and getting good rest.

One very important part of staying healthy is taking care of your **mind**. Having a healthy mind helps us live better lives.

What Is **Mindfulness**?

It can be easy to lose **focus**. We might start doing other things. Or we might start to think about something else.

Mindfulness is about giving our full attention to what we are doing. If you have other thoughts, notice them then turn your attention back to what you are doing.

When we are being mindful, we can use all our **senses** to help us focus.

What Can Mindfulness Do for Us?

Mindfulness helps us learn how to focus better.

Mindfulness can help us keep our minds healthy. It can help us handle **stress** and calm down when we feel nervous.

It doesn't matter where you are or what you are doing. Taking time to be mindful can help.

How Does Mindfulness Work?

It can be easy to worry about things from the past or the future. This can make us miss good things happening now.

Mindfulness helps us focus on what is happening right now. This can help us forget other worries or sad thoughts.

Techniques and Tips

Your bedroom might be a good place for mindfulness.

There are lots of different ways we can be mindful. These are called exercises. Many of them are done best when you are somewhere quiet, calm, and comfy.

Body  Scan

The body scan can help us relax our bodies.

We can learn a lot about how we are feeling from our bodies. Our **muscles** can get very tight when we feel worried.

In the body scan exercise, you move your attention through the different parts of your body. Start at the top of your head and finish on the tips of your toes.

You might find some of your muscles are tight.

15

Take a **Drink**

Focus only on taking a drink.

Grab a drink. It could be juice, water, or anything you'd like. Now, it's time to give all of your attention to that drink.

Think about your drink. Is it hot or cold? How does it smell? How does it taste?

Mindfulness takes lots of practice.

Yoga

In yoga, we make shapes with our bodies. We focus on our breathing and how our bodies are moving.

Drawing

There are lots of ways to be mindful. You could try drawing. The important part is not thinking about what the drawing will be.

Try to notice the feeling of the pencil or crayon on the paper. What colors are you using? What shapes are you drawing?

You could try the same thing while painting!

Calm Kids

Mindfulness is a very good way to keep our minds healthy and calm. If it doesn't work for you, that's okay! There are other ways to take care of your mind.

Glossary

focus	to give your full attention to something
healthy	well and working at your best
mind	the part of a person that thinks, feels, and remembers
muscles	parts of the body that help us to move
senses	the five ways through which we know about the world around us
stress	strong feelings of worry

Index